FOOD LOVERS

TAPAS AND STARTERS

RECIPES SELECTED BY CORINNE MALESIC

Trans
Atlantic
Press

All recipes serve four people, unless otherwise indicated.

For best results when cooking the recipes in this book, buy fresh ingredients and follow the instructions carefully. Make sure that everything is properly cooked through before serving, particularly any meat and shellfish, and note that as a general rule vulnerable groups such as the very young, elderly people, pregnant women, convalescents and anyone suffering from an illness should avoid dishes that contain raw or lightly cooked eggs.

For all recipes, quantities are given in metric measurements followed by standard U.S. cups and imperial measures. Follow one set or the other, but not a mixture of both because conversions may not be exact. Standard spoon and cup measurements are level and are based on the following:

1 tsp = 5 ml, 1 tbsp = 15 ml, 1 cup = 250 ml / 8 fl oz.

Note that Australian standard tablespoons are 20 ml, so Australian readers should use 3 tsp in place of 1 tbsp when measuring small quantities.

The electric oven temperatures in this book are given for conventional ovens with top and bottom heat. When using a fan oven, the temperature should be decreased by about 20–40°F / 10–20°C – check the oven manufacturer's instruction book for further guidance. The cooking times given should be used as an approximate guideline only.

CONTENTS

POTATOES with TOMATO SAUCE   4

FILO PASTRIES with SPINACH and GOAT CHEESE   6

PROSCIUTTO and MANGO SALAD   8

CALAMARI with LIME DRESSING   10

TARRAGON MUSHROOMS on TOAST   12

FRIED CHORIZO with TOMATO and ONION SAUCE   14

CHICKEN KEBABS with PEANUT SAUCE   16

PEARS with BLUE CHEESE and WALNUTS   18

GRILLED PEPPERS with GARLIC   20

TOMATO PUFF PASTRY TARTS   22

ARTICHOKES with RACLETTE CHEESE   24

SHRIMP AND SCALLOPS with LIME SAUCE   26

CHICKEN with BELL PEPPER SAUCE   28

LAMB PASTIES   30

MUSHROOM BRUSCHETTAS   32

ASPARAGUS WRAPPED in PARMA HAM   34

CHICKPEA SALAD with SATAY CHICKEN SKEWERS   36

SHRIMP AND TOMATO KEBABS with THAI SAUCE   38

MUSSELS with PESTO   40

HONEY and MUSTARD CHICKEN WINGS with SESAME SEEDS   42

MEATBALLS with TOMATO SAUCE   44

POTATO TORTILLA   46

POTATOES WITH TOMATO SAUCE

Ingredients

450 g / 1 lb small waxy potatoes, washed

4 tbsp olive oil

2 onions, cut into rings

1 garlic clove

1 red chili pepper, seeds removed and finely chopped

3 tbsp sherry

400 g / 2 cups canned tomatoes

7 tbsp vegetable broth (stock)

100 g / 1 cup black olives, pitted

4 tbsp pine nuts, dry roasted

Salt and freshly ground pepper

Method

Prep and cook time: 25 min

1 Boil the potatoes in salted water for about 20 minutes or until tender.

2 Meanwhile, heat the oil in a pan and gently fry the onion until translucent. Add the garlic and chili and cook for a further 2 minutes.

3 Pour in the sherry, allow to reduce a little then add the tomatoes and vegetable broth (stock). Simmer gently for 10 minutes then season with salt and pepper.

4 Serve the potatoes with the sauce poured over and topped with olives and pine nuts.

FILO PASTRIES WITH SPINACH AND GOAT CHEESE

Ingredients

675 g / 1½ lb spinach, washed and stalks discarded

3 tbsp olive oil

5 scallions (spring onions), finely chopped

¼ tsp grated nutmeg

200 g / 2 cups soft goat cheese, crumbled

450 g / 1 lb filo pastry, thawed if frozen

50 g / ¼ cup butter, melted

Salt and freshly ground pepper

Method

Prep and cook time: 40 min

1 Put the spinach in a large pan. Cover and cook until wilted then drain, squeezing out as much liquid as possible. Finely chop the leaves and set aside.

2 Heat the oil in a pan and gently cook the scallions (spring onions) until soft. Stir in the spinach, nutmeg and goat cheese and cook for 2 minutes. Drain off any liquid, season with salt and pepper and set aside.

3 Heat the oven to 180C (375F / Gas Mark 5).

4 Cut 15 cm x 6 cm (6 inch x 2½ inch) rectangles and brush with melted butter. Put a small spoonful of the mixture on the end of each rectangle and fold 3 times to make a triangular parcel.

5 Place the parcels on a greased baking sheet, brush with more melted butter and bake for 10–15 minutes. Serve hot or cold.

Makes 16

PROSCIUTTO AND MANGO SALAD

Ingredients

5 tbsp olive oil

3 tbsp white wine vinegar

½ tsp chili powder

150 g / 6 oz baby red spinach or beet tops, washed

1 small head radicchio, leaves separated and washed

4 sprigs parsley

1 large mango, peeled, stone removed and sliced

8 slices prosciutto, chopped into strips

Salt and freshly ground pepper

Method

Prep and cook time: 20 min

1 Mix the oil with the vinegar and chili powder, season with salt and pepper and set aside.

2 Arrange the spinach, radicchio leaves and parsley on serving plates.

3 Add the sliced mango and strips of prosciutto and drizzle with the dressing.

4 Serve with any remaining dressing alongside.

CALAMARI WITH LIME DRESSING

Ingredients

1 tbsp white wine vinegar

2 tbsp lime juice

3 tbsp light cream

5 tbsp olive oil

1 tbsp parsley, finely chopped

675 g / 1½ lb calamari rings, thawed if frozen

1 bunch arugula (rocket)

Salt and freshly ground pepper

Lime wedges

Method

Prep and cook time: 20 min

1 Mix the vinegar, lime juice, cream and 3 tbsp of oil to make the dressing. Stir in the parsley, season with salt and pepper and set aside.

2 Heat a griddle pan or broiler (grill) to medium heat. Wash the calamari rings and pat dry. Brush with the remaining oil and cook for about 4 minutes, turning once.

3 Serve the calamari on a bed of arugula (rocket) with the dressing drizzled over and lime wedges to garnish.

TARRAGON MUSHROOMS ON TOAST

Ingredients

4 tbsp butter

250 g / 8 oz button mushrooms

1 garlic clove, finely chopped

½ bunch tarragon, chopped

100 ml / 7 tbsp white wine

4 tbsp crème fraîche

4 slices baguette

Salt and freshly ground pepper

Tarragon leaves, to garnish

Method

Prep and cook time: 10 min

1 Heat the butter in a pan and cook the mushrooms for about 1 minute, or until golden brown.

2 Add the garlic and chopped tarragon, toss briefly and stir in the white wine. Boil until reduced, then stir in the crème fraîche and cook for about 1 minute.

3 Toast the baguette slices on both sides.

4 Season the mushrooms to taste with salt and pepper and place on the toasted baguette slices. Serve garnished with tarragon.

FRIED CHORIZO WITH TOMATO AND ONION SAUCE

Ingredients

6 large tomatoes

125 ml / ½ cup olive oil

250 g / ½ lb cooking chorizo, sliced

1 large onion, chopped

1 garlic clove

2 stalks thyme

Salt and freshly ground pepper

Method

Prep and cook time: 20 min

1 Bring a pan of salted water to a boil and drop in the tomatoes for 30 seconds. Remove from the water, peel and slice. Set aside.

2 Heat 4 tbsp of oil in a wide pan and fry the chorizo slices for about 5 minutes, turning once. Set aside.

3 Heat the remaining oil in the pan and gently cook the onion until soft. Add the garlic, cook for 2 minutes then add the tomatoes.

4 Cover the pan and simmer for 8 minutes, adding a little water if necessary.

5 Add the chorizo and the thyme sprigs and cook for a further 3 minutes. Season with salt and pepper and serve.

CHICKEN KEBABS
WITH PEANUT SAUCE

Ingredients

125 ml / ½ cup sesame oil

1 garlic clove, chopped

2 red chilis, chopped

2 tbsp honey

250 ml / 1 cup smooth peanut butter

1 tbsp soy sauce

1 tsp fish sauce

Juice of 2 limes

2 chicken breasts, skinned and sliced

1 tbsp light oil

Chilis and lime wedges, to garnish

Method

Prep and cook time: 25 min

1 Heat the oil in a small pan and gently cook the garlic and chilis until soft. Stir in the honey, peanut butter, soy sauce, fish sauce and lime juice. Bring to a boil and simmer for 5 minutes.

2 Thread the chicken strips onto wooden skewers and brush with a little oil.

3 Heat a griddle pan and cook the chicken skewers until browned and cooked through.

4 Serve the chicken skewers drizzled with the sauce, garnish with whole chilis and lime wedges, and serve the remaining sauce alongside for dipping.

PEARS WITH BLUE CHEESE AND WALNUTS

Ingredients

6 ripe pears

Juice of ½ a lemon

1 tbsp olive oil

200 g / 2 cups blue cheese, crumbled

150 g / 1½ cups walnuts, chopped

Rosemary sprigs, to garnish

Method

Prep and cook time: 15 min

1 Slice the pears in half lengthways and cut away the cores. Rub the cut surfaces with the lemon juice to prevent browning.

2 Heat the oil in a small pan and add the crumbled blue cheese and the walnuts.

3 Stir over a gentle heat until the cheese has just melted then spoon the mixture into the core cavities of the pears.

4 Serve immediately garnished with the rosemary.

GRILLED PEPPERS WITH GARLIC

Ingredients

6 long red bell peppers

125 ml / ½ cup olive oil

Juice of ½ a lemon

6 cloves new season garlic,
roughly chopped

10 g / ½ cup parsley, roughly chopped

Salt and freshly ground pepper

Method

Prep and cook time: 40 min

1 Put the whole bell peppers under a hot broiler (grill), turning frequently, until the skins are charred all over.

2 Place the peppers in a large bowl, cover with plastic wrap (clingfilm) and let cool for 15 minutes.

3 Remove and discard the skins, stalks and seeds from the peppers.

4 Blend the olive oil with the lemon juice, season with salt and pepper, and mix well with the peppers.

5 Arrange on a serving plate and scatter with the garlic and parsley. For a gentler flavor, fry the garlic in a little olive oil until soft before adding to the dish. If no new season garlic is available, do the same with stored garlic.

TOMATO PUFF PASTRY TARTS

Ingredients

4 tbsp olive oil

4 garlic cloves, sliced

450 g / 1 lb all-butter puff pastry, thawed if frozen

450 g / 1 lb tomatoes, sliced

Salt and freshly ground pepper

Parsley, to garnish

Method

Prep and cook time: 40 min

1 Heat the oven to 180C (375F / Gas Mark 5).

2 Heat 3 tbsp of oil in a small pan and gently cook the garlic until softened.

3 Roll out the pastry to a thickness of 1 cm / ¼ inch, cut 10 cm / 4 inch diameter circles and place on a greased cookie sheet. Leaving a 1½ cm / ½ inch rim, score an inner circle on the pastry and carefully remove the top two layers of pastry from the inner circle.

4 Lay the sliced tomatoes in the middle of the tarts, scatter over the fried garlic and drizzle over the remaining oil.

5 Season with salt and pepper and bake for 15–20 minutes or until golden brown. Serve garnished with parsley.

ARTICHOKES WITH RACLETTE CHEESE

Ingredients

4 globe artichokes

1 tbsp white wine vinegar

2 tbsp olive oil

2 garlic cloves, chopped

8 slices raclette cheese

1 tbsp chopped parsley

Salt and freshly ground pepper

Method

Prep and cook time: 35 min

1 Slice the artichokes in half vertically. Remove the tough outer leaves, peel the stalks and scrape out the hairy chokes with a teaspoon.

2 Bring a large pan of water to a boil with the vinegar and boil the prepared artichokes for 10–15 minutes or until tender. Drain well and set aside.

3 Heat the oven to 240C (475F / Gas Mark 9).

4 Place the artichokes cup side up in an ovenproof dish. Drizzle over the oil, scatter with the garlic and season with salt and pepper.

5 Lay one slice of cheese on each artichoke, sprinkle with the parsley and bake for 5 minutes or until the cheese is melted and golden brown. Serve hot or warm.

SHRIMP AND SCALLOPS WITH LIME SAUCE

Ingredients

Juice and zest of 4 limes

1 tbsp fish sauce

1 tsp sugar

8 scallops, with shells

3 tbsp olive oil

2 garlic cloves, finely chopped

1 red chili, seeds removed and finely chopped

8 large shrimps (prawns), tails and black veins removed

Method

Prep and cook time: 20 min

1 Mix the lime juice and zest with the fish sauce and sugar and set aside.

2 Cut the scallops away from the shell, discarding the corals. Rinse the scallops and shells and pat dry with kitchen paper. Slice each scallop in half horizontally and set aside.

3 Heat the oil in a skillet and gently fry the garlic and chili until just starting to soften. Remove the garlic and chili with a slotted spoon and add to the lime juice mixture.

4 Place the scallops cut side down in the skillet and cook for 1 minute on each side. Remove from the skillet and add to the lime juice mixture.

5 Heat the skillet again, quickly fry the shrimps (prawns) until cooked through and add to the lime and scallop mixture.

6 Place two halves of a scallop on each shell along with one shrimp and pour over the lime mixture.

CHICKEN WITH BELL PEPPER SAUCE

Ingredients

125 ml / ½ cup oil

Juice of 2 limes

2 tbsp honey

1 red chili, seeds removed and chopped

2 chicken breasts, skinned

2 orange bell peppers

1 garlic clove

Salt and freshly ground pepper

Lime zest, to garnish

Method

Prep and cook time: 45 min

1 Whisk together 6 tbsp of oil with the lime juice, honey and chopped chili to make a marinade.

2 Cut the chicken into bite-size pieces, mix with the marinade and set aside.

3 Brush the bell peppers with a little oil and place under a hot broiler (grill) until the skins are charred all over, turning frequently. Put in a bowl, cover with plastic wrap (clingfilm) and set aside.

4 Heat 2 tbsp of oil in a pan and gently fry the garlic for 2 minutes.

5 Remove and discard the pepper skins and seeds. Place the peppers in a food processor with the garlic and blend well. Season with salt and pepper and set aside.

6 Remove the chicken from the marinade. Heat the remaining oil in a skillet and fry the chicken pieces for about 6 minutes or until browned on all sides and cooked through.

7 Mix the peppers and garlic with the reserved marinade, briskly bring to a boil in the skillet then turn down the heat for a few minutes. Drizzle over the chicken pieces. Scatter with lime zest and serve immediately.

LAMB PASTIES

Ingredients

For the pastry:

50 g / ¼ cup butter, chopped

250 g / 2½ cups all-purpose (plain) flour

3 tbsp olive oil

½ tsp salt

For the filling:

3 tbsp oil

1 onion, finely chopped

2 garlic cloves, chopped

250 g / 9 oz ground (minced) lamb

150 g / 1½ cups feta cheese, crumbled

1 tbsp pine nuts, chopped

2 egg yolks

Oil, for brushing

Salt and freshly ground pepper

Method

Prep and cook time: 50 min

1 Rub the butter into the flour until the mixture resembles breadcrumbs. Add the oil, salt and enough water to make a dough. Wrap in plastic wrap (clingfilm) and chill for 20 minutes.

2 Meanwhile, make the filling. Heat the oil in a pan and gently cook the onion until translucent. Add the garlic and lamb and cook, stirring, until the meat is well browned.

3 Remove from the heat and stir in the feta cheese, pine nuts and egg yolks. Season with salt and pepper and set aside.

4 Heat the oven to 180C (375F / Gas Mark 5).

5 Roll out the pastry thinly and cut circles about 10 cm/4 inches in diameter with a cutter. Place a little filling on each circle, moisten the edge with a little water, fold over to form semi-circles and press the join closed with a fork.

6 Place the pasties on a greased cookie sheet, brush with a little oil and bake for 15–20 minutes or until golden brown.

Makes 20

MUSHROOM BRUSCHETTAS

Ingredients

4 tbsp olive oil

1 small onion, finely chopped

1 garlic clove, crushed

200 g / 2 cups button mushrooms, finely chopped

50 g / 1 cup black olives, pitted and finely chopped

12 slices baguette, toasted

Salt and freshly ground pepper

2 tbsp parsley, finely chopped, to garnish

Method

Prep and cook time: 25 min

1 Heat 3 tbsp of oil in a pan and gently fry the onion until soft.

2 Add the garlic, cook for 1 minute then add the mushrooms and cook for 10 minutes. Stir in the olives and season with salt and pepper.

3 Brush the toasted bread with the remaining oil, spoon over the mushroom mixture and garnish with the chopped parsley.

ASPARAGUS WRAPPED IN PARMA HAM

Ingredients

20 asparagus spears

50 g / ¼ cup butter, melted

10 slices Parma ham, sliced in half lengthways

Salt

Method

Prep and cook time: 15 min

1 Trim the bases off the asparagus and boil in a large pan of salted water for 4 minutes or until just tender.

2 Drizzle the asparagus with the melted butter and roll each one up in a strip of Parma ham.

CHICKPEA SALAD WITH SATAY CHICKEN SKEWERS

Ingredients

3 tbsp smooth peanut butter

125 ml / ½ cup olive oil

1 tbsp honey

Juice of 1 lime

2 chicken breasts, skinned and cut into strips

800 g / 4 cups canned chickpeas, drained and rinsed

2 red onion, finely chopped

2 red chilis, seeds removed and finely chopped

25 g / 1 cup chopped parsley

Juice of 1 lemon

Salt and freshly ground pepper

Method

Prep and cook time: 15 min plus 30 to marinate

1 Blend the peanut butter with 2 tbsp of oil, the honey and the lime juice. Pour over the chicken strips, mix well and set aside for 30 minutes.

2 Mix the chickpeas with the chopped onion, chilis and parsley. Mix the remaining oil with the lemon juice, season with salt and pepper and pour over the chickpeas.

3 Remove the chicken strips from the marinade and thread onto wooden skewers.

4 Cook the chicken under a hot broiler (grill) for 5 minutes or until cooked through, turning once. Serve with the chickpea salad.

SHRIMP AND TOMATO KEBABS WITH THAI SAUCE

Ingredients

6 tbsp soy sauce

2 tbsp fish sauce

3 tbsp sesame oil

Juice of 2 limes

2 tbsp honey

2 red chilis, seeds removed and finely chopped

2 garlic cloves, finely chopped

2 scallions (spring onions), finely chopped

675 g / 1½ lb large shrimps (prawns), tails and black veins removed

450 g / 1 lb cherry tomatoes, halved

Lime wedges, to garnish

Method
Prep and cook time: 20 min plus 30 min to marinate

1 Mix the soy sauce, fish sauce, 2 tbsp of sesame oil, the lime juice and honey in a large bowl.

2 Add the chopped chilis, garlic and scallions (spring onions) and mix in the shrimps (prawns). Set aside to marinate for 30 minutes, turning from time to time.

3 Heat the broiler (grill) to a medium setting.

4 Remove the shrimps from the marinade, brush the tomato halves with the remaining oil and thread onto wooden skewers alternating with the shrimps.

5 Heat the marinade in a small pan until reduced and slightly sticky. Set aside.

6 Cook the kebabs under the broiler, turning frequently, for about 6 minutes or until the shrimps are cooked through.

7 Serve the kebabs with the warm marinade drizzled over and lime wedges to garnish.

MUSSELS WITH PESTO

Ingredients

900 g / 2 lb mussels, scraped clean
and beards removed

125 ml / ½ cup white wine

25 g / 1 oz Parmesan cheese, grated

For the pesto:

50 g / 2 oz basil leaves

2 tbsp pine nuts

1 garlic clove, crushed

2 tbsp Parmesan cheese, grated

125 ml / ½ cup olive oil

Salt and freshly ground pepper

Method
Prep and cook time: 40 min

1 First make the pesto: pulse the basil, pine nuts
and garlic in a food processor, or pound in a pestle
and mortar, until coarsely chopped. Stir in the
Parmesan cheese and olive oil and season with salt
and pepper.

2 Tap each mussel against the side of the sink as
you wash them and discard any that remain open.

3 Place the mussels in a large pan with the white
wine and half a cup of water. Cover with a lid and
cook over a medium heat for about 7 minutes,
shaking the pan from time to time.Discard any
mussels that remain closed after cooking.

4 Heat the oven to 220C (425F / Gas Mark 7).

5 Break off the top shell of each mussel and
discard. Place the mussels on an ovenproof serving
dish and spoon a little pesto onto each one. Sprinkle
with the grated Parmesan cheese and heat in the
oven for 3 minutes.

HONEY AND MUSTARD CHICKEN WINGS WITH SESAME SEEDS

Ingredients

3 tbsp olive oil

4 tbsp honey

2 tbsp Dijon mustard

Juice of 1 lemon

12 chicken wings

4 tbsp sesame seeds

Salt and freshly ground pepper

Method

Prep and cook time: 30 min plus 1 hour to marinate

1 Whisk together the oil, honey, mustard and lemon juice to make a maarinade. Season with salt and pepper.

2 Put the chicken wings into a large bowl, pour over the marinade and mix well. Set aside for at least 1 hour, turning from time to time.

3 Heat the oven to 200C (400F / Gas Mark 6).

4 Toast the sesame seeds in a dry skillet until lightly browned. Set aside.

5 Remove the chicken wings from the marinade and put onto a cookie sheet. Roast in the oven for 15–20 minutes, turning once, until cooked through and browned all over.

6 Sprinkle the chicken wings with the toasted sesame seeds and serve warm or cold.

MEATBALLS
WITH TOMATO SAUCE

Ingredients

For the sauce:

2 tbsp olive oil

1 onion, finely chopped

1 garlic clove, finely chopped

1 bay leaf

400 g / 2 cups canned tomatoes, chopped

1 tbsp tomato paste (purée)

Salt and freshly ground pepper

For the meatballs:

1 slice white bread, soaked in a little water

450 g / 1 lb ground (minced) beef

1 egg, beaten

1 garlic clove, crushed

2 red chilis, seeds removed and finely chopped

1 onion, finely chopped

1 tsp dried thyme

2 tbsp chopped parsley

Salt and freshly ground pepper

Oil, for frying

1 garlic clove, finely chopped, to serve (optional)

Method
Prep and cook time: 40 min

1 To make the sauce, heat the oil in a pan and gently fry the onion until translucent.

2 Add the garlic, cook for 1 minute then add the bay leaf, tomatoes and tomato paste (purée). Stir in half a cup of water and let simmer for 15–20 minutes. Season with salt and pepper and remove from the heat.

3 Meanwhile, make the meatballs. Squeeze the excess liquid out of the bread and mix with the other meatball ingredients. Season with salt and pepper and shape into balls.

4 Heat 2 tbsp of oil in a skillet and fry the meatballs for about 10 minutes, shaking the skillet so they cook on all sides. Add more oil as necessary.

5 Remove the bay leaf from the sauce and discard. Spoon a little sauce into paper cases and top with a meatball. Serve garnished with raw chopped garlic (optional).

POTATO TORTILLA

Ingredients

4 medium waxy potatoes, peeled

6 eggs

1 tbsp thyme, finely chopped

2 tbsp parsley, finely chopped

4 tbsp olive oil

Salt and freshly ground pepper

Method

Prep and cook time: 50 min

1 Boil the potatoes in a large pan of salted water until just tender. Let cool a little, cut in half lengthways and slice.

2 Beat the eggs in a large bowl, add the herbs, season with salt and pepper and add the sliced potatoes.

3 Heat 2 tbsp of oil over a medium flame in a 20 cm / 8 inch skillet (frying pan) and pour in half the egg / potato mixture.

4 Let cook for about 3 minutes then place a large plate over the pan, carefully invert and slide the tortilla, uncooked side down, back into the skillet.

5 Continue cooking for 2 more minutes or until the mixture is set then remove the tortilla from the pan.

6 Repeat with the remaining oil and egg / potato mixture. Slice the tortillas and serve warm or cold.

Published by Transatlantic Press

First published in 2011

Transatlantic Press
38 Copthorne Road, Croxley Green, Hertfordshire WD3 4AQ

© Transatlantic Press

Images and Recipes by StockFood © The Food Image Agency

Recipes selected by Corinne Malesic, StockFood

A catalogue record for this book is available from the British Library.

ISBN 978-1-908533-62-3

Printed in China